Desserts

- Introduction — 2
- Frugal Cakes — 4
- Prudent Pies & Tarts — 22
- Budget Bars — 40
- Thrifty Desserts — 62
- Index — 80

Eating Well. Spending Less.

With a growing number of people feeling the pinch of tightening budgets, eating out and convenience cooking can be a financial drain. Fortunately, home-cooked meals are often more delicious and better for you than processed foods. Rediscover the pleasure of cooking at home with this collection of budget-friendly dessert recipes that will help you eat well and save money.

DOING THE MATH

Every recipe in this collection was individually priced to determine the cost per serving. Keep in mind that food costs vary regionally and seasonally, so exact prices per serving are not included. For budget planning, each recipe is marked with either the 99¢ or Less icon or the Budget Friendly icon next to the recipe title.

 Per serving, this recipe does not cost more than 99¢ to make.

 Per serving, this recipe does not cost more than $1.99 to make.

- All calculations are based on actual grocery store prices. The least expensive ingredients available were chosen, including some store-brand products and sale items.

- Prices include all ingredients as listed in the recipe, except salt, pepper, and ingredients labeled as "optional."

- If a range is offered for the amount of an ingredient ($1/8$ teaspoon to $1/4$ teaspoon, for example), the smaller amount was used to calculate the cost per serving.

- If an ingredient is presented with an option ($3/4$ cup chopped tomatoes or red bell peppers, for example), the first item listed was used to calculate the cost per serving.

- If there is a range of serving sizes (makes 4 to 6 servings, for example), the larger number of servings was used to calculate the cost per serving.

- Food shown in the photo that is not listed as an ingredient (including garnishes, optional items and serving suggestions) was not included in the cost per serving.

Inspired recipes and smart shopping are all it takes to create delicious sweet treats that won't break your budget. You'll be amazed at how easy and affordable it is to skip the supermarket pastry case and make your own irresistible desserts at home.

SHOPPING SMARTER

- Planning ahead is the easiest way to save money. Supermarkets often offer special prices on baking staples like flour, sugar, eggs and butter around the holidays. If you know you'll be baking a lot, check the ads in your area, clip coupons and stock up. Tightly wrapped, butter can be frozen for 6 to 9 months. All-purpose flour and cake mixes can be stored in a cool, dry place for up to a year. Granulated sugar and brown sugar will keep indefinitely if kept away from high humidity.

- Out of season, fresh fruits can be prohibitively expensive. Frozen fruits, picked and packaged during their regular growing season, offer the same great flavor and nutritional benefits for much less. Also, consider buying extra fruit in season, when prices are at their lowest, and freezing it for use later in the year.

- Nuts can often be one of the most expensive ingredients in delicious desserts. Make the most of nuts by chopping them for more even distribution, toasting them to maximize flavor and buying in bulk. Most nuts will keep at least 3 months when stored in an airtight container in the refrigerator and even longer when frozen. Chopped pecans and walnuts are often more expensive, so look for shelled halves instead and do the chopping yourself.

- Choose convenience products wisely. While you will definitely pay a premium for products like prepared pie crusts, cake mixes and canned pie fillings, the time savings can often be significant. If you have the time, you can learn how to make these things from scratch for even greater savings.

- Choose less expensive generic or store-brand products when shopping for baking ingredients like flour, sugar, baking soda, butter, nuts and eggs. You won't notice any difference and the savings can add up quickly.

- Don't buy spices in large quantities. Spices like cinnamon, nutmeg and allspice are most flavorful immediately after they are ground and become dull as time passes. Buying spices in small quantities may seem more expensive, but just a little goes a long way. You can also purchase spices whole to save money and grind them as needed so that none goes to waste.

Frugal Cakes

Butterscotch Bundt Cake

- 1 package (about 18 ounces) yellow cake mix *without pudding in the mix*
- 1 package (4-serving size) butterscotch instant pudding and pie filling mix
- 1 cup water
- 3 eggs
- 2 teaspoons ground cinnamon
- ½ cup chopped pecans
- Powdered sugar (optional)

1. Preheat oven to 325°F. Spray 12-cup bundt pan with nonstick cooking spray.

2. Beat cake mix, pudding mix, water, eggs and cinnamon in large bowl with electric mixer at medium speed 2 minutes or until blended. Stir in pecans. Pour batter into prepared pan.

3. Bake 40 to 50 minutes or until cake springs back when lightly touched. Cool in pan on wire rack 10 minutes. Invert cake onto serving plate; cool completely. Sprinkle with powdered sugar, if desired.

Makes 12 servings

Pistachio Walnut Bundt Cake: Substitute white cake mix for yellow cake mix, pistachio pudding mix for butterscotch pudding mix and walnuts for pecans.

Chocolate Strawberry Cream Cake

- 2 cups plus 3 tablespoons sugar, divided
- 2 cups all-purpose flour
- ½ cup unsweetened cocoa powder
- 2 teaspoons baking soda
- ½ teaspoon salt
- 1 cup warm water
- ½ cup (1 stick) butter, melted
- ½ cup vegetable oil
- ½ cup buttermilk
- 2 eggs, at room temperature
- 3 teaspoons vanilla, divided
- 1½ cups plus 3 tablespoons whipping cream, divided
- 1 cup (6 ounces) semisweet chocolate chips
- ½ cup strawberry jam
- 3 tablespoons sour cream
- Fresh strawberries (optional)

1. Preheat oven to 350°F. Spray two 9-inch round cake pans with nonstick cooking spray. Line bottoms of pans with waxed paper or parchment paper; spray with cooking spray.

2. Whisk 2 cups sugar, flour, cocoa, baking soda and salt in large bowl. Beat water, butter, oil, buttermilk, eggs and 2 teaspoons vanilla in medium bowl with electric mixer at medium-high speed until well blended; add flour mixture. Beat at low speed 2 minutes. Pour batter into prepared pans.

3. Bake 35 to 40 minutes or until toothpick inserted into centers comes out clean. Cool in pans 15 minutes. Remove to wire racks; cool completely.

4. Meanwhile, place 3 tablespoons whipping cream and chocolate chips in small microwavable bowl; microwave on HIGH 40 seconds. Stir until smooth. Cool to spreading consistency.

5. Place 1 cake layer on serving plate. Spread top with jam. Spread cooled chocolate mixture over jam. Top with remaining cake layer. Cover loosely; refrigerate 2 hours or up to 2 days.

6. Beat remaining 1½ cups whipping cream, 3 tablespoons sugar, 1 teaspoon vanilla and sour cream in large bowl with electric mixer at medium-high speed just until stiff peaks form. (Do not overbeat.) Spread top and side of cake with frosting. Refrigerate cake until ready to serve, up to 8 hours. Garnish with strawberries.

Makes 12 servings

Tip: To make slicing the cake easier and neater, use a knife that has been dipped in hot water and wipe it clean after each slice.

Celebration Pumpkin Cake

- 1 package (about 18 ounces) spice cake mix
- 1 can (15 ounces) solid-pack pumpkin
- 3 eggs
- ¼ cup (½ stick) butter, softened
- 1½ containers (16 ounces each) cream cheese frosting
- ⅓ cup caramel ice cream topping
- 1 cup pecan halves

1. Preheat oven to 350°F. Grease and flour three 9-inch round cake pans.

2. Beat cake mix, pumpkin, eggs and butter in large bowl with electric mixer at medium speed 2 minutes. Pour batter into prepared pans.

3. Bake 20 to 25 minutes or until toothpick inserted into centers comes out clean. Cool in pans 15 minutes. Remove to wire racks; cool completely.

4. Place 1 cake layer on serving plate; spread with frosting. Top with remaining cake layer. Frost top and side of cake. Spread caramel topping over top of cake, letting some caramel drip down side. Decorate with pecan halves.   *Makes 12 servings*

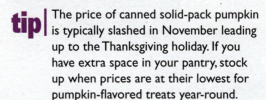

tip | The price of canned solid-pack pumpkin is typically slashed in November leading up to the Thanksgiving holiday. If you have extra space in your pantry, stock up when prices are at their lowest for pumpkin-flavored treats year-round.

Chocolatey Bananas Foster Cake

- 1 package (about 18 ounces) devil's food cake mix
- 1 cup mashed bananas*
- 3 eggs
- ⅓ cup vegetable oil
- ¼ cup water
- ¼ cup packed brown sugar
- 2 tablespoons butter
- ¾ cup finely chopped firm ripe bananas
- ½ teaspoon rum extract (optional)
- ¼ teaspoon ground cinnamon
- 2 cups whipping cream
- ¼ cup powdered sugar

Overripe bananas provide the most intense banana flavor.

1. Preheat oven to 350°F. Coat two 8-inch round cake pans with nonstick cooking spray.

2. Beat cake mix, mashed bananas, eggs, oil and water in medium bowl with electric mixer at low speed 30 seconds. Beat at medium speed 2 minutes. Pour batter into prepared pans. Bake 23 to 25 minutes or until toothpick inserted into centers comes out clean. Cool in pans 15 minutes. Remove to wire racks; cool completely.

3. Combine brown sugar and butter in small saucepan over medium-low heat; cook and stir until smooth. Stir in chopped bananas, rum extract, if desired, and cinnamon. Cook and stir until mixture thickens slightly. Cool completely.

4. Beat cream and powdered sugar in medium bowl with electric mixer at high speed until stiff peaks form.

5. Place 1 cake layer on serving plate. Spread top with half of whipped cream; spoon banana mixture evenly over whipped cream. Top with remaining cake layer. Spread top and side with remaining whipped cream. Store leftovers in refrigerator.

Makes 12 servings

Frugal Cakes

Blueberry Crumb Cake

Crumb Topping (recipe follows)
2 cups all-purpose flour
2/3 cup sugar
1 tablespoon baking powder
1 teaspoon salt
1/2 teaspoon baking soda
1 cup milk
1/2 cup (1 stick) butter, melted
2 eggs, beaten
2 tablespoons lemon juice
2 cups thawed frozen blueberries

try other berries

1. Preheat oven to 375°F. Grease 13×9-inch baking pan. Prepare Crumb Topping; set aside.

2. Sift flour, sugar, baking powder, salt and baking soda into large bowl. Combine milk, butter, eggs and lemon juice in medium bowl. Pour into flour mixture; stir until blended.

3. Pour batter into prepared pan. Sprinkle blueberries evenly over batter; sprinkle with Crumb Topping.

4. Bake 40 to 45 minutes or until toothpick inserted into center comes out clean. Serve warm. *Makes 12 to 15 servings*

Crumb Topping: Combine 1 cup chopped walnuts, 2/3 cup sugar, 1/2 cup all-purpose flour, 1/4 cup (1/2 stick) softened butter and 1/2 teaspoon ground cinnamon in large bowl until mixture forms coarse crumbs. Makes about 2 1/2 cups.

Frugal Cakes 13

Rich Chocolate Torte

1 cup (2 sticks) plus 2 tablespoons unsalted butter, softened, divided
8 ounces bittersweet chocolate, chopped
4 eggs
1¼ cups sugar
⅓ cup cornstarch
1 tablespoon water
1 tablespoon vanilla
Unsweetened cocoa powder (optional)

1. Preheat oven to 350°F. Melt 2 tablespoons butter; brush on bottom and side of 9-inch springform pan. Wrap outside of pan with foil.

2. Place chocolate in small microwavable bowl. Microwave on HIGH 30 seconds; stir. Microwave at additional 15-second intervals until chocolate is melted and smooth; cool slightly.

3. Beat remaining 1 cup butter in medium bowl with electric mixer at medium-high speed until light and fluffy. Add cooled chocolate; beat at medium speed 2 minutes. Beat eggs in large bowl; gradually add sugar. Beat at high speed 5 minutes or until mixture is pale and thick. Sift cornstarch over egg mixture and stir to blend. Add chocolate mixture, water and vanilla; beat just until blended. Pour batter into prepared pan.

4. Place springform pan in large roasting pan. Place in oven; add 1 inch hot water to roasting pan.

5. Bake 40 minutes or until center is set. Remove springform pan from roasting pan; cool completely on wire rack. Remove side of pan and invert onto serving plate. Remove bottom of pan by sliding thin knife or spatula underneath to release. (Torte may be wrapped and refrigerated up to 3 days before serving.) Sift cocoa over top, if desired.

Makes 12 servings

Variation: For a coffee-flavored torte, dissolve 1 tablespoon instant coffee granules in 2 tablespoons water. Add to batter with chocolate mixture instead of 1 tablespoon water and vanilla.

Frugal Cakes 15

Pecan Spice Cake with Browned Butter Frosting

- 1 package (about 18 ounces) yellow cake mix with pudding in the mix
- ¾ cup water
- ¾ cup sour cream
- 3 eggs
- 1 tablespoon grated lemon peel
- 1½ teaspoons ground cinnamon
- ½ teaspoon ground nutmeg
- ¼ teaspoon ground allspice
- 1 cup chopped pecans
- Browned Butter Frosting (recipe follows)
- Additional chopped pecans (optional)

1. Preheat oven to 350°F. Grease two 9-inch square baking pans.

2. Beat cake mix, water, sour cream, eggs, lemon peel, cinnamon, nutmeg and allspice in large bowl with electric mixer at low speed 30 seconds. Beat at high speed 2 minutes. Stir in 1 cup pecans. Pour batter into prepared pans.

3. Bake 25 to 30 minutes or until toothpick inserted into centers comes out clean. Cool in pans 15 minutes. Remove to wire racks; cool completely.

4. Prepare Browned Butter Frosting. Place 1 cake layer on serving plate. Spread with one third of frosting. Top with remaining cake layer. Frost top and sides of cake with remaining frosting. Sprinkle with additional pecans, if desired. Store tightly covered at room temperature.

Makes 12 servings

Browned Butter Frosting

¾ cup (1½ sticks) butter
5½ cups sifted powdered sugar
1½ teaspoons vanilla
Dash salt
8 to 9 tablespoons whipping cream or half-and-half

Melt butter in small, heavy saucepan over medium heat; cook and stir until butter is light amber in color. Cool butter slightly. Combine browned butter, powdered sugar, vanilla, salt and 8 tablespoons cream in large bowl. Beat at medium speed until smooth and of spreading consistency. Stir in additional 1 tablespoon cream if frosting is too stiff.

White Chocolate Cake

- 2 cups all-purpose flour
- 2¼ teaspoons baking powder
- ½ teaspoon salt
- 1 cup milk
- ½ cup (1 stick) butter
- 4 ounces white chocolate, broken into pieces
- 1½ cups sugar
- 4 eggs
- 1 teaspoon vanilla
- 12 ounces bittersweet chocolate, chopped
- 1¼ cups whipping cream
- White chocolate curls (optional)

1. Preheat oven to 350°F. Grease two 9-inch round cake pans.

2. Combine flour, baking powder and salt in medium bowl. Combine milk, butter and white chocolate in medium saucepan; cook and stir over medium-low heat until smooth.

3. Beat sugar and eggs in large bowl with electric mixer at medium speed 3 minutes or until pale and thick. Add vanilla; beat until blended. Slowly add flour mixture, beating until well blended. Slowly beat in milk mixture. Pour batter into prepared pans.

4. Bake 24 to 28 minutes or until toothpick inserted into centers comes out clean. Cool in pans 15 minutes. Remove to wire racks; cool completely.

5. Place bittersweet chocolate in medium bowl. Heat cream in small saucepan over medium-low heat until bubbles appear around edge of pan. (Do not boil.) Pour over chocolate; let stand 2 minutes. Stir until chocolate is melted and smooth. Let stand 15 minutes or until thick enough to spread.

6. Place 1 cake layer on serving plate; spread with one third of bittersweet chocolate mixture. Top with remaining cake layer; spread top and side of cake with remaining mixture. Garnish with white chocolate curls.

Makes 12 servings

Frugal Cakes

Toasted Almond Supreme

- 1 package (about 18 ounces) devil's food cake mix, plus ingredients to prepare mix
- 2 teaspoons instant coffee granules
- 2 cups whipping cream
- ¾ cup powdered sugar
- 2 tablespoons unsweetened cocoa powder
- 1½ teaspoons vanilla
- ½ cup seedless raspberry jam
- 1 cup sliced almonds, toasted*
- Fresh raspberries (optional)

*To toast almonds, spread in single layer on baking sheet. Bake in preheated 350°F oven 5 to 7 minutes or until golden brown, stirring occasionally.

1. Preheat oven to 350°F. Lightly grease two 9-inch round cake pans. Line bottoms of pans with waxed paper. Prepare cake mix according to package directions, adding coffee granules. Pour batter into prepared pans; bake according to package directions. Cool in pans 15 minutes. Remove to wire racks; cool completely.

2. Beat cream in medium bowl with electric mixer at high speed 2 minutes or until soft peaks form. Add powdered sugar, cocoa and vanilla; beat 20 seconds or until stiff peaks form. Cover; refrigerate until ready to use.

3. Place 1 cake layer on serving plate. Spread top with half of jam. Repeat layers. Spread top and side of cake with whipped cream mixture.

4. Sprinkle half of almonds over top of cake; press remaining almonds onto side of cake. Cover loosely; refrigerate until ready to serve. Decorate with raspberries just before serving, if desired.

Makes 12 servings

Frugal Cakes

Prudent Pies & Tarts

Cherry Frangipane Tart

- ½ (15-ounce) package refrigerated pie crusts
- ⅔ cup slivered almonds
- ½ cup all-purpose flour
- ¼ cup powdered sugar
- ½ cup (1 stick) butter, softened
- 2 eggs
- 1¾ cups pitted frozen sweet cherries
- Fresh mint (optional)

1. Preheat oven to 450°F. Line tart pan with pie crust; cover with parchment paper. Fill with dried beans or pie weights and bake 10 minutes. Remove from oven. Carefully remove paper and weights.

2. *Reduce oven temperature to 350°F.* Combine almonds, flour and powdered sugar in food processor; process until finely ground. Add butter; pulse to blend. Add eggs, 1 at a time, while processor is running. Pour into crust; smooth top. Sprinkle with cherries.

3. Bake 35 minutes or until set. Cool completely in pan on wire rack. Garnish with mint. *Makes 8 servings*

Classic Apple Pie

99¢ or LESS

- 1 package (15 ounces) refrigerated pie crusts
- 6 cups sliced Granny Smith apples (about 6 medium)
- ½ cup sugar
- 1 tablespoon cornstarch
- 2 teaspoons lemon juice
- ½ teaspoon ground cinnamon
- ½ teaspoon vanilla
- ⅛ teaspoon salt
- ⅛ teaspoon ground nutmeg
- ⅛ teaspoon ground cloves
- 1 tablespoon whipping cream

1. Preheat oven to 350°F. Line 9-inch pie pan with 1 pie crust. (Keep remaining pie crust in refrigerator while preparing apples.)

2. Combine apples, sugar, cornstarch, lemon juice, cinnamon, vanilla, salt, nutmeg and cloves in large bowl; mix well. Pour into prepared crust. Place remaining crust over apples; crimp edge to seal.

3. Cut 4 slits in top crust; brush with cream. Bake 40 minutes or until crust is golden brown. Cool slightly before serving.

Makes 8 servings

Easy Cherry Cream Pie

1 pint vanilla ice cream, softened
½ (16-ounce) package frozen dark sweet cherries, chopped
1 cup whipping cream
1 tablespoon powdered sugar
⅛ teaspoon almond extract
1 (6-ounce) chocolate crumb or graham cracker pie crust

1. Combine ice cream and cherries in large bowl just until blended.

2. Beat cream, powdered sugar and almond extract in medium bowl with electric mixer at medium speed until soft peaks form.

3. Spoon ice cream mixture into pie crust. Spread evenly with whipped cream mixture. Freeze 1 hour or until firm. Let stand at rooom temperature 10 minutes before serving. *Makes 8 servings*

 This luscious pie couldn't be easier to make and can be altered to fit whatever happens to be on sale. If frozen berries are less expensive, substitute an equal amount for the frozen cherries and use vanilla extract instead of almond extract.

Sweet Coconut Custard Pie

99¢ or LESS

- ½ (15-ounce) package refrigerated pie crusts
- 1 cup sugar
- 1 tablespoon cornstarch
- 4 eggs
- ¾ cup buttermilk
- ¼ cup (½ stick) butter, melted and cooled
- 1 teaspoon vanilla
- ¼ teaspoon salt
- 1 cup shredded coconut

1. Preheat oven to 350°F. Let pie crust stand at room temperature 15 minutes. Line 9-inch pie pan with pie crust.

2. Combine sugar and cornstarch in large bowl; mix well. Add eggs, buttermilk, butter, vanilla and salt; whisk until smooth. Stir in coconut. Pour mixture into crust.

3. Bake 45 to 50 minutes or until set. Cool completely in pan on wire rack.

Makes 8 servings

tip To save even more money, substitute powdered or dry buttermilk for the fresh buttermilk in this recipe. It costs less because it does not have to be refrigerated until after opening, plus it prevents waste. Following the directions on the package, blend the powder with water to create exactly the amount of buttermilk you need.

Prudent Pies & Tarts

Rustic Plum Tart

99¢ or LESS

- ¼ cup (½ stick) plus 1 tablespoon butter, divided
- 3 cups plum wedges (about 6 medium, see Tip)
- ¼ cup granulated sugar
- ½ cup all-purpose flour
- ½ cup uncooked old-fashioned or quick oats
- ¼ cup packed brown sugar
- ½ teaspoon ground cinnamon
- ¼ teaspoon salt
- 1 egg
- 1 teaspoon water
- ½ (15-ounce) package refrigerated pie crusts
- 1 tablespoon chopped crystallized ginger (optional)

1. Preheat oven to 425°F. Line baking sheet with parchment paper.

2. Melt 1 tablespoon butter in large skillet over high heat. Add plums; cook and stir 3 minutes or until plums are softened. Stir in granulated sugar; cook 1 minute or until juices have thickened. Remove from heat; set aside.

3. Combine flour, oats, brown sugar, cinnamon and salt in medium bowl. Cut in remaining ¼ cup butter with pastry blender or 2 knives until mixture resembles coarse crumbs.

4. Beat egg and water in small bowl. Unroll pie crust on prepared baking sheet. Brush crust lightly with egg mixture. Sprinkle with ¼ cup oat mixture, leaving 2-inch border around edge of crust. Drain plums; spoon plums over oat mixture. Sprinkle with ginger. Fold crust edge up around plums, overlapping as necessary. Sprinkle with remaining oat mixture. Brush edge of crust with egg mixture.

5. Bake 25 minutes or until golden brown. Cool slightly before serving.

Makes 8 servings

Tip: For this recipe, use dark reddish-purple plums and cut each into 8 wedges.

Prudent Pies & Tarts 31

Pumpkin Pecan Pie

1 can (15 ounces) solid-pack pumpkin
1 can (14 ounces) sweetened condensed milk
¼ cup (½ stick) butter, softened
2 eggs, divided
1 teaspoon ground cinnamon
1 teaspoon vanilla
½ teaspoon ground nutmeg
¼ teaspoon salt
1 (6-ounce) graham cracker pie crust
2 tablespoons packed brown sugar
2 tablespoons dark corn syrup
1 tablespoon butter, melted
½ teaspoon maple flavoring (optional)
1 cup chopped pecans

1. Preheat oven to 400°F.

2. Combine pumpkin, sweetened condensed milk, softened butter, 1 egg, cinnamon, vanilla, nutmeg and salt in large bowl; beat until well blended. Pour into crust. Bake 20 minutes. *Reduce oven temperature to 350°F.*

3. Beat remaining egg, brown sugar, corn syrup, melted butter and maple flavoring, if desired, in medium bowl with electric mixer at medium speed until well blended. Stir in pecans.

4. Pour pecan mixture over pumpkin layer. Bake 25 minutes or until knife inserted near center comes out clean. *Makes 8 servings*

Custard Peach Tart

99¢ or LESS

1 cup all-purpose flour
¼ teaspoon plus ⅛ teaspoon salt, divided
¼ cup (½ stick) butter, cut into pieces
2 to 3 tablespoon water
1 egg, separated
2 eggs
3 tablespoons sugar
1 teaspoon vanilla
¼ teaspoon ground nutmeg
1 cup milk
1 package (12 ounces) frozen unsweetened peach slices, thawed and drained

1. Preheat oven to 400°F. Combine flour and ¼ teaspoon salt in medium bowl. Cut in butter with pastry blender or 2 knives until mixture resembles coarse crumbs. Stir in 2 tablespoons water just until moistened, adding additional water if necessary. Form dough into disc.

2. Roll out dough into 11-inch circle on lightly floured surface. Place dough in 9-inch tart pan with removable bottom. Turn under edge of dough. Pierce bottom and side of dough with fork. Beat egg white; lightly brush egg white onto bottom and side of crust. Discard any remaining egg white. Place tart pan on cookie sheet. Bake 10 minutes. Cool in pan on wire rack.

3. Meanwhile, whisk egg yolk, 2 eggs, sugar, vanilla, nutmeg and remaining ⅛ teaspoon salt in large bowl until blended. Microwave milk 1 minute on HIGH or until hot. (Do not boil.) Whisk milk into egg mixture until blended. Arrange peach slices in crust; pour egg mixture over peaches.

4. Bake 25 to 27 minutes or until set. Cool completely in pan on wire rack. Refrigerate at least 2 hours or overnight. *Makes 8 servings*

Prudent Pies & Tarts 35

Mocha Cappuccino Ice Cream Pie

99¢ or Less

- ¼ cup cold water
- 1 tablespoon instant coffee granules
- 2 tablespoons sugar
- ½ teaspoon vanilla
- 4 cups fudge marble ice cream, softened
- 1 (6-ounce) graham cracker pie crust

1. Combine water, coffee granules, sugar and vanilla in small bowl; stir until granules dissolve.

2. Combine ice cream and coffee mixture in large bowl; stir gently until well blended. Spoon into pie crust; smooth top.

3. Cover; freeze 4 hours or until firm. Let stand at room temperature 10 minutes before serving.

Makes 8 servings

tip | This ice cream pie is the perfect weeknight dessert. It comes together in minutes and since it is stored in the freezer, you never have to worry about the pie becoming stale before you can enjoy the last piece.

Chocolate Walnut Toffee Tart

    2 cups all-purpose flour
1¼ cups plus 3 tablespoons sugar, divided
    ¾ cup (1½ sticks) butter, cut into pieces
    2 egg yolks
1¼ cups whipping cream
    1 teaspoon ground cinnamon
    2 teaspoons vanilla
    2 cups coarsely chopped walnuts
1¼ cups semisweet chocolate chips or chunks, divided

1. Line bottom of oven with foil to catch any spills. Preheat oven to 325°F. Place flour and 3 tablespoons sugar in food processor; process using on/off pulsing action just until mixed. Add butter; process 20 seconds. Add egg yolks; process 10 seconds (mixture may be crumbly).

2. Press dough evenly into ungreased 10-inch tart pan with removable bottom. Bake 10 minutes or until surface is no longer shiny.

3. *Increase oven temperature to 375°F.* Combine remaining 1¼ cups sugar, cream and cinnamon in large saucepan; bring to a boil. Reduce heat to medium-low; simmer 10 minutes, stirring frequently. Remove from heat; stir in vanilla.

4. Sprinkle walnuts and 1 cup chocolate chips evenly over crust. Pour cream mixture over top. Bake 35 to 40 minutes or until filling is bubbly and crust is lightly browned. Cool completely in pan on wire rack.

5. Place remaining ¼ cup chocolate chips in small resealable food storage bag. Microwave on HIGH 20 seconds; knead bag until chocolate is melted. Cut small hole in one corner of bag; drizzle chocolate over tart. *Makes 10 servings*

Note: Tart may be made up to 5 days in advance. Cover and store at room temperature.

Budget Bars

Chewy Peanut Butter Brownies

¾ cup (1½ sticks) butter, melted
¾ cup creamy peanut butter
1¾ cups sugar
2 teaspoons vanilla
4 eggs
1¼ cups all-purpose flour
½ teaspoon baking powder
¼ teaspoon salt
¼ cup unsweetened cocoa powder

1. Preheat oven to 350°F. Grease 13×9-inch baking pan.

2. Beat butter and peanut butter in large bowl with electric mixer at low speed 3 minutes or until well blended. Add sugar and vanilla; beat until blended. Add eggs, 1 at a time, beating until blended after each addition. Stir in flour, baking powder and salt just until blended. Reserve 1¾ cups batter. Stir cocoa into remaining batter.

3. Spread chocolate batter in prepared pan. Top with reserved batter. Bake 30 minutes or until edges begin to pull away from sides of pan. Cool completely in pan on wire rack. Cut into bars.

Makes 2 dozen brownies

Cranberry Coconut Bars

99¢ or LESS

- 2 cups thawed frozen cranberries
- 1 cup dried sweetened cranberries
- ⅔ cup granulated sugar
- ¼ cup water
- Grated peel of 1 lemon
- 1¼ cups all-purpose flour
- ¾ cup uncooked old-fashioned oats
- ½ teaspoon baking soda
- ½ teaspoon salt
- 1 cup packed light brown sugar
- ¾ cup (1½ sticks) unsalted butter, softened
- 1 cup chopped pecans, toasted*
- 1 cup shredded sweetened coconut

To toast pecans, spread in single layer on baking sheet. Bake in preheated 350°F oven 5 to 7 minutes or until golden brown, stirring frequently.

1. Preheat oven to 400°F. Grease and flour 13×9-inch baking pan.

2. Combine cranberries, dried cranberries, granulated sugar, water and lemon peel in medium saucepan. Cook over medium-high heat 10 to 15 minutes or until mixture is pulpy, stirring frequently. Mash cranberries with back of spoon. Cool to room temperature.

3. Combine flour, oats, baking soda and salt in medium bowl. Beat brown sugar and butter in large bowl with electric mixer at medium speed until creamy. Add flour mixture; beat just until blended. Stir in pecans and coconut. Reserve 1½ cups; press remaining crumb mixture into bottom of prepared pan. Bake 10 minutes.

4. Gently spread cranberry mixture evenly over crust. Sprinkle with reserved crumb mixture. Bake 18 to 20 minutes or until center is set and top is golden brown. Cool completely in pan on wire rack. Cut into bars.

Makes 2 dozen bars

Pumpkin Streusel Bars

1 cup granulated sugar
1 cup solid-pack pumpkin
½ cup vegetable oil
2 eggs
2 tablespoons unsalted butter, melted
1½ cups all-purpose flour, divided
1½ teaspoons baking powder
1 teaspoon ground cinnamon
¼ teaspoon salt
¼ teaspoon baking soda
⅛ teaspoon ground ginger
½ cup packed light brown sugar
¼ cup (½ stick) unsalted butter, cubed
1 cup coarsely chopped pecans

1. Preheat oven to 350°F. Grease 13×9-inch baking pan.

2. Beat granulated sugar, pumpkin, oil, eggs and melted butter in large bowl with electric mixer at medium speed until well blended. Combine 1 cup flour, baking powder, cinnamon, salt, baking soda and ginger in small bowl. Gradually add flour mixture to pumpkin mixture, beating after each addition. Spread batter in prepared pan.

3. Combine remaining ½ cup flour and brown sugar in large bowl. Cut in ¼ cup butter with pastry blender or 2 knives until mixture resembles coarse crumbs. Stir in pecans; sprinkle evenly over batter.

4. Bake 35 minutes or until toothpick inserted into center comes out clean. Cool completely in pan on wire rack. Cut into bars.

Makes 2 dozen bars

Budget Bars 45

Java Cream Brownie Bars

1 package (about 19 ounces) brownie mix, plus ingredients to prepare mix
¼ cup seedless raspberry jam
1 cup whipping cream, divided
4 ounces semisweet chocolate chips
¼ cup powdered sugar
1 teaspoon instant coffee granules

1. Preheat oven to 350°F. Line 9-inch square baking pan with double layer of foil, allowing 2-inch overhang around all sides.

2. Prepare brownie mix according to package directions; pour batter into prepared pan. Bake 35 minutes or until toothpick inserted into center comes out clean. Cool completely in pan on wire rack.

3. Melt jam in medium saucepan over medium heat, stirring frequently. Brush evenly over cooled brownies. Bring ½ cup cream to a simmer in same saucepan over medium heat. (Do not boil.) Remove from heat; stir in chocolate chips until melted and smooth. Pour chocolate mixture evenly over top; let cool.

4. Combine 2 tablespoons cream and instant coffee; stir until completely dissolved. Beat remaining cream in medium bowl with electric mixer at medium-high speed until soft peaks form. Gradually add coffee mixture and powdered sugar; beat until stiff peaks form. Spread over brownies. Refrigerate until ready to serve. Remove foil; cut into bars.

Makes 16 bars

Budget Bars

Chocolate Walnut Bars

1½ cups all-purpose flour
¾ cup sugar
¾ cup (1½ sticks) butter
1 can (14 ounces) sweetened condensed milk
1 cup semisweet chocolate chips
1 egg, beaten
½ teaspoon vanilla
2 cups walnuts, toasted and chopped

1. Preheat oven to 350°F. Combine flour and sugar in large bowl; cut in butter with pastry blender or 2 knives until mixture resembles coarse crumbs. Press into bottom of ungreased 13×9-inch baking pan. Bake 20 minutes or until lightly browned.

2. Meanwhile, combine sweetened condensed milk and chocolate chips in medium saucepan. Cook and stir over low heat until smooth. Remove from heat; cool slightly.

3. Add egg and vanilla to chocolate mixture; stir until well blended. Stir in walnuts. Spread chocolate mixture over crust. Bake 25 minutes or until set. Cool completely in pan on wire rack. Cut into bars.

Makes 2 dozen bars

Raspberry Almond Squares

99¢ or LESS

- 1 package (about 18 ounces) yellow cake mix
- ½ cup sliced almonds, coarsely chopped
- ½ cup (1 stick) butter, melted
- 1 jar (12 ounces) seedless raspberry jam
- 1 package (8 ounces) cream cheese, softened
- 2 tablespoons all-purpose flour
- 1 egg

1. Preheat oven to 350°F. Line 13×9-inch baking pan with foil, allowing 2-inch overhang around all sides.

2. Beat cake mix, almonds and butter in large bowl with electric mixer at medium speed until crumbly. Reserve 1 cup mixture; press remaining mixture into bottom of prepared pan. Bake 10 to 12 minutes or until light golden brown.

3. Spread jam evenly over baked crust. Beat cream cheese, flour and egg at medium speed until combined. Spread over jam; top with reserved crumb mixture.

4. Bake 18 to 20 minutes or until light golden brown. Cool completely in pan on wire rack. Remove foil; cut into bars.

Makes 2 dozen bars

Cocoa Bottom Banana Pecan Bars

99¢ or LESS

- 1 cup sugar
- ½ cup (1 stick) butter, softened
- 5 ripe bananas, mashed
- 1 egg
- 1 teaspoon vanilla
- 1½ cups all-purpose flour
- 1 teaspoon baking powder
- 1 teaspoon baking soda
- ½ teaspoon salt
- ½ cup chopped pecans
- ¼ cup unsweetened cocoa powder

1. Preheat oven to 350°F. Grease 13×9-inch baking pan.

2. Beat sugar and butter in large bowl with electric mixer at medium speed until creamy. Add bananas, egg and vanilla; beat until well blended. Combine flour, baking powder, baking soda and salt in medium bowl. Add to banana mixture; beat until well blended. Stir in pecans.

3. Divide batter in half. Stir cocoa into one half. Spread chocolate batter in prepared pan. Top with remaining batter; swirl with knife.

4. Bake 30 to 35 minutes or until edges are lightly browned. Cool completely in pan on wire rack. Cut into bars. *Makes 2 dozen bars*

Triple Chocolate Cream Cheese Bars

99¢ or LESS

- 1 package (about 18 ounces) chocolate cake mix
- ⅓ cup vegetable oil
- 3 eggs, divided
- 2 packages (8 ounces each) cream cheese, softened
- ⅓ cup sugar
- 1 cup sour cream
- 1 cup (6 ounces) semisweet chocolate chips, melted and cooled slightly
- 1 cup white chocolate chips

1. Preheat oven to 350°F. Grease 13×9-inch baking pan.

2. Combine cake mix, oil and 1 egg in medium bowl; mix well. Press into bottom of prepared baking pan. Bake 10 minutes or until set.

3. Beat cream cheese in large bowl with electric mixer at high speed until light and fluffy. Add remaining 2 eggs and sugar; beat until well blended. Beat in sour cream and melted chocolate until blended. Pour mixture over crust; sprinkle with white chocolate chips.

4. Bake 50 minutes or until set. Cool completely in pan on wire rack. Refrigerate until chilled. Cut into bars.

Makes 2 dozen bars

Coconut Lime Bars

99¢ or LESS

- 1 package (about 18 ounces) white cake mix
- 1 cup coconut, toasted*
- ½ cup (1 stick) butter, melted
- 1 can (14 ounces) sweetened condensed milk
- 1 package (8 ounces) cream cheese, softened
- Grated peel and juice of 3 limes
- 3 eggs
- Additional toasted coconut (optional)

*To toast coconut, heat small nonstick skillet over medium heat. Add coconut; cook and stir 5 to 7 minutes or until golden brown. Immediately remove from heat to prevent burning.

1. Preheat oven to 350°F. Line 13×9-inch pan with foil, allowing 2-inch overhang around all sides.

2. Combine cake mix, coconut and butter in large bowl until crumbly. Press mixture into bottom of prepared pan. Bake 12 minutes or until light golden brown.

3. Beat sweetened condensed milk, cream cheese, lime peel and juice in another large bowl with electric mixer at medium speed 2 minutes or until well blended; scrape down sides of bowl. Beat in eggs, 1 at a time, until well blended. Spread mixture evenly over crust.

4. Bake 20 minutes or until center is set and edges are lightly browned. Sprinkle with additional coconut, if desired. Cool completely in pan on wire rack. Remove foil; cut into bars.

Makes about 2 dozen bars

Gingerbread Cheesecake Bars

1 package (8 ounces) cream cheese, softened
⅔ cup sugar, divided
3 eggs, divided
1½ teaspoons ground ginger, divided
½ teaspoons vanilla
½ cup (1 stick) butter, softened
¾ cup molasses
2 cups all-purpose flour
1 teaspoon baking soda
¾ teaspoon ground cinnamon
¼ teaspoon salt
¼ teaspoon ground allspice

1. Preheat oven to 350°F. Grease 13×9-inch baking pan.

2. Beat cream cheese and ⅓ cup sugar in medium bowl with electric mixer at medium speed until light and fluffy. Add 1 egg, ½ teaspoon ginger and vanilla; beat until well blended and smooth. Refrigerate until ready to use.

3. Beat butter and remaining ⅓ cup sugar in large bowl at medium speed until light and fluffy. Add molasses and remaining 2 eggs; beat until well blended. Combine flour, baking soda, remaining 1 teaspoon ginger, cinnamon, salt and allspice in small bowl. Add flour mixture to butter mixture; beat just until blended. Spread batter evenly in prepared pan. Drop cream cheese mixture by spoonfuls onto gingerbread batter; swirl with knife.

4. Bake 25 to 30 minutes or until toothpick inserted into center comes out clean. Cool completely in pan on wire rack. Cut into bars.

Makes 2 dozen bars

Budget Bars

Creamy Lemon Bars

- 1 package (about 18 ounces) white or yellow cake mix with pudding in the mix
- 2 eggs, divided
- ⅓ cup vegetable oil
- 1 package (8 ounces) cream cheese, softened
- ⅓ cup sugar
- 1 teaspoon lemon juice

1. Preheat oven to 350°F.

2. Combine cake mix, 1 egg and oil in large bowl until crumbly. Reserve 1 cup crumb mixture. Press remaining crumb mixture into bottom of ungreased 13×9-inch baking pan. Bake 15 minutes or until light golden brown.

3. Beat cream cheese, sugar, remaining egg and lemon juice in medium bowl with electric mixer at medium speed until smooth and well blended. Spread over crust. Sprinkle with reserved crumb mixture.

4. Bake 15 minutes or until set. Cool completely in pan on wire rack. Cut into bars.

Makes 2 dozen bars

Thrifty Desserts

Chocolate Mousse

- 1 package (8 ounces) semisweet chocolate chips
- 6 tablespoons unsalted butter
- ¼ cup brewed strong coffee
- 3 eggs, separated
- ½ cup whipping cream
- ¼ cup superfine sugar
- Sweetened whipped cream (optional)

1. Combine chocolate chips, butter and coffee in large saucepan; cook and stir over low heat until smooth. Whisk in egg yolks, 1 at a time, until well blended. Remove from heat; cool slightly.

2. Beat cream in small bowl with electric mixer at high speed until soft peaks form. Refrigerate until ready to use.

3. Beat egg whites in medium bowl until soft peaks form. Add sugar, 1 tablespoon at a time, beating until stiff peaks form.

4. Fold egg whites into whipped cream mixture. Fold in cooled chocolate mixture. Cover and chill 4 hours. Garnish with sweetened whipped cream. *Makes 6 servings*

Apple Crumble Pot

- 1 cup plus 2 tablespoons biscuit baking mix, divided
- 1 cup packed dark brown sugar, divided
- 1½ teaspoons ground cinnamon
- ¼ teaspoon ground allspice
- 4 Granny Smith apples (about 2 pounds), cored and cut into 8 wedges each
- ½ cup dried cranberries
- 5 tablespoons butter, cut into pieces, divided
- 1 teaspoon vanilla
- ½ cup rolled oats
- ½ cup chopped pecans

Slow Cooker Directions

1. Coat slow cooker with nonstick cooking spray. Combine 2 tablespoons baking mix, ⅔ cup brown sugar, cinnamon and allspice in large bowl. Add apples, cranberries, 2 tablespoons butter and vanilla; toss gently to coat. Transfer to slow cooker.

2. Combine remaining 1 cup baking mix, oats and remaining ⅓ cup brown sugar in medium bowl. Cut in remaining 3 tablespoons butter with pastry blender or 2 knives until mixture resembles coarse crumbs. Sprinkle evenly over apple mixture. Top with pecans. Cover; cook on HIGH 2 hours or until apples are tender.

3. Turn off slow cooker. Let stand, uncovered, 15 to 30 minutes before serving.

Makes 6 servings

Easy Peach Buckle

1 package (16 ounces) frozen peach slices
¾ cup water
1 tablespoon granulated sugar
¾ cup plus 2 tablespoons all-purpose flour
¼ cup packed brown sugar
1 teaspoon baking powder
¾ teaspoon ground cinnamon
½ teaspoon baking soda
⅛ teaspoon salt
⅔ cup buttermilk
3 tablespoons vegetable oil
½ teaspoon vanilla

1. Preheat oven to 375°F. Lightly grease 1½-quart baking dish.

2. Combine peaches and water in medium saucepan; bring to a boil. Reduce heat to medium-low; simmer 3 minutes. Remove from heat; stir in granulated sugar.

3. Combine flour, brown sugar, baking powder, cinnamon, baking soda and salt in medium bowl. Combine buttermilk, oil and vanilla in small bowl; mix well. Stir into flour mixture just until blended.

4. Spread batter evenly in prepared baking dish. Spoon peach mixture over batter. Bake 30 minutes or until lightly browned and cake springs back when touched. Serve warm.

Makes 6 servings

Thrifty Desserts

Blackberry Panna Cotta

- 1 package (12 ounces) frozen unsweetened blackberries, thawed
- 2 cups whipping cream
- 1 cup buttermilk
- ¾ cup sugar
- 3 tablespoons water
- 1 envelope (1 ounce) unflavored gelatin

1. Process blackberries in food processor or blender until smooth. Combine cream, buttermilk and sugar in medium saucepan over medium heat. Add blackberry purée. Bring to a simmer over low heat.

2. Pour water into small saucepan. Sprinkle with gelatin; heat over low heat, swirling pan until gelatin is dissolved. Pour into blackberry mixture; stir until combined.

3. Strain mixture through fine mesh sieve or strainer, pressing down with rubber spatula. Pour evenly into 6 (8-ounce) ramekins or custard cups. Refrigerate 6 hours or until set. To serve, unmold onto serving plates.

Makes 6 servings

tip | This creamy custard will delight with its rich fruity flavor and silky texture. Served cold, it is particularly refreshing in the warmer summer months.

Thrifty Desserts 69

Apricot Soufflé

99¢ or less

- 3 tablespoons butter
- 2 tablespoons all-purpose flour
- ¾ cup apricot fruit spread
- ⅓ cup finely chopped dried apricots
- ¼ cup water
- 3 egg yolks, beaten
- 4 egg whites
- ¼ teaspoon cream of tartar
- ⅛ teaspoon salt

1. Preheat oven to 325°F. Melt butter in medium saucepan. Add flour; cook and stir until bubbly. Add fruit spread, apricots and water; cook and stir 3 minutes or until thickened. Remove from heat; whisk in egg yolks. Cool to room temperature, stirring occasionally.

2. Beat egg whites, cream of tartar and salt in medium bowl with electric mixer at high speed until stiff peaks form. Gently fold into apricot mixture. Spoon into 1½-quart soufflé dish. Bake 30 minutes or until puffed and golden brown.* Serve immediately.

Makes 6 servings

*Soufflé will be soft in center. For a firmer soufflé, increase baking time to 35 minutes.

tip | Soufflés have an undeserved reputation for being overly fancy and difficult to make. In fact, once you see how this delicious soufflé comes together in just a few easy steps, you'll want to make it all the time.

Chocolate Cherry Turnovers

1 package (8 ounces) refrigerated crescent roll dough
¾ cup semisweet chocolate chips, divided
½ cup canned cherry pie filling

1. Preheat oven to 375°F. Line baking sheet with parchment paper.

2. Unroll dough onto clean work surface; separate into 4 rectangles. Press perforations firmly to seal. Cut off corners of rectangles with sharp paring knife to form oval shapes.

3. Place 1 tablespoon chocolate chips on half of each oval; top with 2 tablespoons pie filling. Sprinkle with additional 1 tablespoon chocolate chips. Fold dough over filling; press edges to seal. Crimp edges with fork, if desired.

4. Bake 15 minutes or until golden brown. Cool on baking sheet 5 minutes. Melt remaining chocolate chips and drizzle over turnovers. Serve warm.

Makes 4 turnovers

Cran-Raspberry Chill

1 can (16 ounces) whole berry cranberry sauce
1 package (12 ounces) frozen unsweetened raspberries
2 cans (12 ounces each) ginger ale, divided

1. Place cranberry sauce, raspberries and 1 can ginger ale in blender; blend until smooth.

2. Place mixture in large resealable food storage bag. Add remaining can ginger ale; seal and shake to blend. Freeze overnight.

3. Crush frozen cranberry mixture in bag until slushy. Serve immediately.

Makes 8 servings

Thrifty Desserts

Rice Pudding with Berries

1½ cups water
¾ cup quick-cooking brown rice
½ cup dried cranberries
1¾ cups milk
1 package (4-serving size) vanilla instant pudding and pie filling mix
½ teaspoon ground cinnamon
⅛ teaspoon salt
1 cup frozen blueberries, thawed
1 tablespoon powdered sugar
¼ teaspoon vanilla

1. Combine water, rice and cranberries in medium saucepan; bring to a boil. Reduce heat to medium-low; simmer, covered, 12 minutes or until water is absorbed and rice is tender.

2. Whisk milk, pudding mix, cinnamon and salt in medium bowl 2 minutes or until thickened. Add cooked rice to pudding mixture; stir well.

3. Combine blueberries, powdered sugar and vanilla in small bowl; toss gently to coat. Serve rice pudding with blueberry mixture.

Makes 6 servings

Thrifty Desserts 75

Peach-Raspberry Cobbler with Corn Bread Biscuits

- 1 package (16 ounces) frozen unsweetened sliced peaches, thawed
- 1 cup frozen raspberries
- 1/3 cup orange juice
- 1/4 cup packed brown sugar
- 1/3 cup plus 2 tablespoons all-purpose flour, divided
- 1/8 teaspoon ground allspice
- 3 tablespoons yellow cornmeal
- 1 tablespoon granulated sugar
- 1 teaspoon baking powder
- 1/4 teaspoon salt
- 2 tablespoons butter
- 1 egg
- 3 tablespoons milk

1. Preheat oven to 400°F. Combine peaches, raspberries, orange juice, brown sugar, 2 tablespoons flour and allspice in large bowl. Spoon about 1/2 cup peach mixture into each of 6 (8-ounce) custard cups or ramekins.

2. Combine remaining 1/3 cup flour, cornmeal, granulated sugar, baking powder and salt in large bowl. Cut in butter with pastry blender or 2 knives until mixture resembles coarse crumbs. Whisk egg and milk in small bowl. Stir egg mixture into flour mixture just until moistened. Spoon evenly over peach mixture. Bake 20 to 25 minutes or until toothpick inserted into topping comes out clean. *Makes 6 servings*

 # Orange Granita

- 6 small oranges
- ¼ cup sugar
- ¼ cup water
- ⅛ teaspoon cinnamon
- Fresh mint (optional)

1. Cut oranges in half; squeeze juice into medium bowl and reserve empty shells. Strain juice to remove seeds, if necessary. Combine sugar and water in small microwavable bowl; microwave on HIGH 30 seconds or until sugar is dissolved. Stir sugar mixture and cinnamon into juice.

2. Pour juice mixture into 9-inch baking pan. Cover and place on flat surface in freezer. After 1 to 2 hours when ice crystals form at edges, stir with fork. Stir 2 or 3 more times at 20 to 30 minute intervals until texture is like icy snow.

3. Scoop granita into orange shells to serve. Garnish with mint.

Makes 6 servings

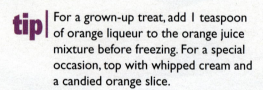 For a grown-up treat, add 1 teaspoon of orange liqueur to the orange juice mixture before freezing. For a special occasion, top with whipped cream and a candied orange slice.

Thrifty Desserts

A
Apple Crumble Pot, 64
Apricot Soufflé, 70

B
Blackberry Panna Cotta, 68
Blueberry Crumb Cake, 12
Browned Butter Frosting, 17
Butterscotch Bundt Cake, 4

C
Celebration Pumpkin Cake, 8
Cherry Frangipane Tart, 22
Chewy Peanut Butter Brownies, 40
Chocolate Cherry Turnovers, 72
Chocolate Mousse, 62
Chocolate Strawberry Cream Cake, 6
Chocolate Walnut Bars, 48
Chocolate Walnut Toffee Tart, 38
Chocolatey Bananas Foster Cake, 10
Classic Apple Pie, 24
Cocoa Bottom Banana Pecan Bars, 52
Coconut Lime Bars, 56
Cranberry Coconut Bars, 42
Cran-Raspberry Chill, 72
Creamy Lemon Bars, 60
Crumb Topping, 12
Custard Peach Tart, 34

E
Easy Cherry Cream Pie, 26
Easy Peach Buckle, 66

G
Gingerbread Cheesecake Bars, 58

J
Java Cream Brownie Bars, 46

M
Mocha Cappuccino Ice Ceam Pie, 36

O
Orange Granita, 78

P
Peach-Raspberry Cobbler with Corn Bread Biscuits, 76
Pecan Spice Cake with Browned Butter Frosting, 16
Pistachio Walnut Bundt Cake, 4
Pumpkin Pecan Pie, 32
Pumpkin Streusel Bars, 44

R
Raspberry Almond Squares, 50
Rice Pudding with Berries, 74
Rich Chocolate Torte, 14
Rustic Plum Tart, 30

S
Sweet Coconut Custard Pie, 28

T
Toasted Almond Supreme, 20
Triple Chocolate Cream Cheese Bars, 54

W
White Chocolate Cake, 18